Happ[y]
2021 from the
Society.   Love You

MW01615386

Consider the

Lilies

WALNUT SPRINGS PRESS

Cover Design by Tracy Anderson (tracyandersonphoto.com)
Cover illustration by 123rf.com

Interior illustrations by Mandy Atkin (instagram.com/mandy.atkin.art), except
photographs on pages 2, 14, 51, and 58, and illustrations on pages 1, 5, 6, 8–9, 12–13,
15, 18, 25, 26–27, 35, 39, 43, 44–45, 47, 48–49, 52–53, and 56, all by 123rf.com. All
small watercolor embellishments by 123rf.com.

ISBN-13: 978-1-59992-249-2

Printed in China.

Consider the lilies of the field, how they grow; they toil not, neither do they spin;

And yet I say unto you, that even Solomon in all his glory was not arrayed like one of these.

Wherefore, if God so clothe the grass of the field, which to day is, and to morrow is cast into the oven, even so will he clothe you, if ye are not of little faith.

JST Matthew 6:28-30

The goodness of God
is infinitely more wonderful
than we will ever be able
to comprehend.

AIDEN WILSON TOZER

By saying that the once-wise king [Solomon] in all his glory was not arrayed like one of the lilies, we are to understand that the flush of colorful spring anemones scattered over all the hills, valleys, and plains would produce in the eyes of the beholder genuine admiration and awe for the elegant beauty of one of God's simple creations. If God cares for the smallest works of his hands, surely he will care for and provide for humankind, his crowning creation.

D. Kelly Ogden

The possession of all the gold and silver in the world would not satisfy the cravings of the immortal soul of man. The gift of the Holy Spirit of the Lord alone can produce a good, wholesome, contented mind. Instead of looking for gold and silver, look to the heavens and try to learn wisdom until you can organize the native elements for your benefit; then, and not until then, will you begin to possess the true riches.

Brigham Young

Trusting God completely
means having faith
that He knows
what is best for your life.
You expect Him
to keep His promises,
help you with problems,
and do the impossible
when necessary.

RICK WARREN

$\mathcal{G}$od is too good to be unkind,

and He is too wise to be mistaken.

And when we cannot trace His

hand, we must trust His heart.

Charles Haddon Spurgeon

The world would have you believe that you are of worth only if you have money, a certain physical appearance, stylish clothes, or social position. The gospel assures you that your value is not dependent on your looks or material possessions. What matters are the beliefs you have in your heart. Part of what it means to be a Latter-day Saint is to know within your soul your eternal worth, who you really are, and why you are here on earth.

Elaine L. Jack

*G*od knows what you need. He knows what is best for you—including in what quantity. The fact is, we can live with very little, but we can never truly live without God. He is what we need first, foremost, and always. He is the only one whom we truly can't do without!

Charles Stanley

The "world" is our opportunity to prove ourselves. This is a part of the great plan of the Lord, to be confronted with the things of the "world," that we might overcome them and be strengthened.

James A. Cullimore

Your Heavenly Father loves you—
each of you. That love never changes.
It is not influenced by your appearance,
by your possessions, or by the amount
of money you have in your bank account.
It is not changed by your talents and
abilities. It is simply there. It is there
for you when you are sad or happy,
discouraged or hopeful. God's love is
there for you whether or not you feel
you deserve love. It is simply always there.

Thomas S. Monson

The *goodness of God*
is the highest object of prayer,
and it reaches down
to *our lowest need.*

Julian of Norwich

Overcome the world, and do
not be led astray by the fashions
and practices of those whose
interests are centered upon
the things of this world.

Joseph Fielding Smith

God is God.
He knows
what he is doing.

MAX LUCADO

Heavenly Father and His Son,

Jesus Christ, are perfect. . . .

Their hopes for us are perfect.

Their plan for us is perfect,

and their promises are sure.

Carole M. Stephens

And shewing mercy
unto thousands of them that love me,
and keep my commandments.

Exodus 20:6

The great thing to remember is that though our feelings come and go, God's love for us does not.

C. S. Lewis

It seems evident that the Lord is afflicted each time we are afflicted, that he will send angels to help us, and that in his love he helps us daily, whether we know it or not. How our hearts ought to be drawn out in gratitude for the grace of the Father and the Son!

Gene R. Cook

We women have a lot to learn about simplifying our lives. We have to decide what is important and then move along at a pace that is comfortable for us. We have to develop the maturity to stop trying to prove something. We have to learn to be content with what we are.

Marjorie Pay Hinckley

$\mathcal{L}$et us consider the lily in the field. It is buried in the ground with a root, which strikes out in the darkness to receive strength and moisture from the soil; and soon a stalk pushes its way through the earth, and pushes it up and up until finally the lily blooms in the sunshine and produces its kind. So man lives on the earth. His tentacles are his hands; his nervous system, his brain. From the earth he produces his living. For what purpose? That he, too, might realize the ideal—not the gratification of the appetite; not the gratification of passions; but that the spirit might move in the sunshine of the Holy Ghost; that he might be, as Peter said, a "partaker of the divine nature."

David O. McKay

Oh, how great is the goodness of God, greater than we can understand. There are moments and there are mysteries of the divine mercy over which the heavens are astounded. Let our judgment of souls cease, for God's mercy upon them is extraordinary.

Mary Faustina Kowalska

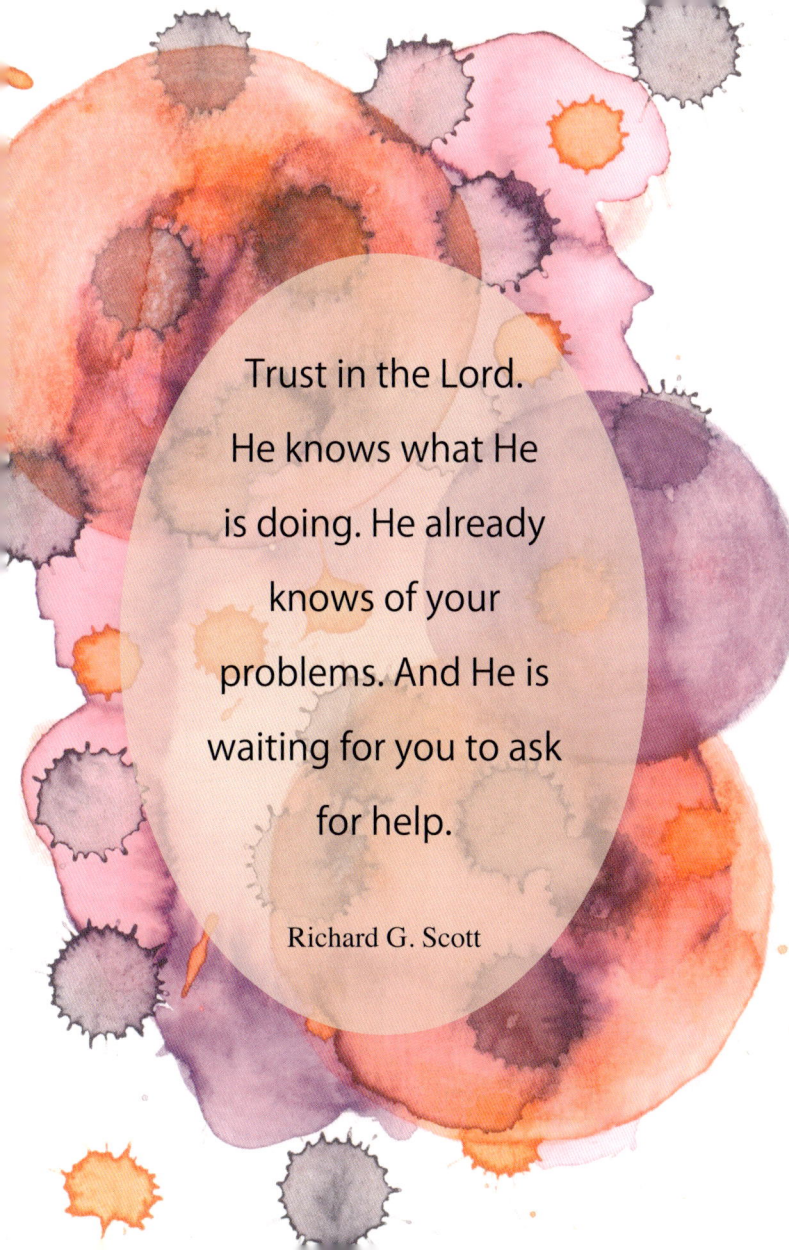

Trust in the Lord.
He knows what He
is doing. He already
knows of your
problems. And He is
waiting for you to ask
for help.

Richard G. Scott

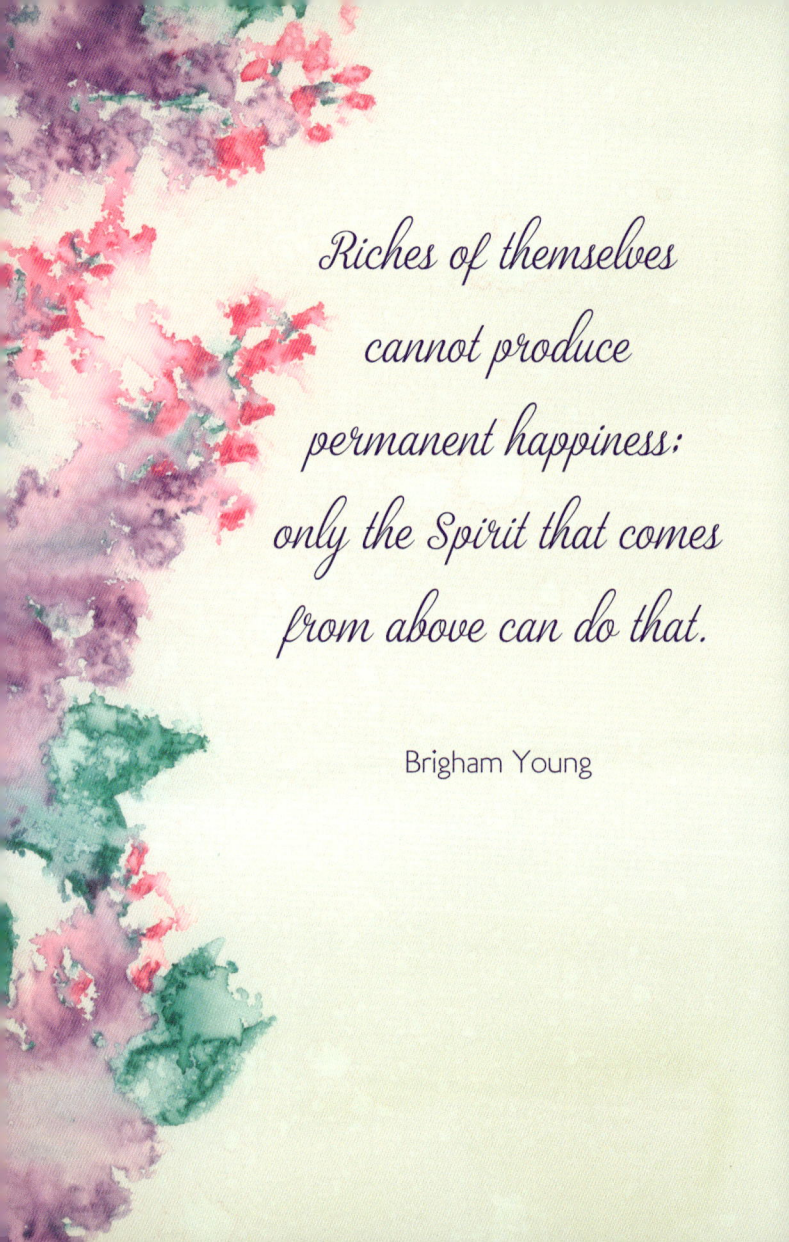

Riches of themselves
cannot produce
permanent happiness:
only the Spirit that comes
from above can do that.

Brigham Young

Love not the world,
neither the things that
are in the world. If any
man love the world,
the love of the Father
is not in him.

1 John 2:15

Perhaps at no other time do we feel

the divine love of the Savior

as abundantly as we do

when we repent and

feel His loving arms

outstretched to embrace us

and assure us of

His love and acceptance.

LINDA S. REEVES

This is true faith, a
living confidence in
the goodness of God.

Martin Luther

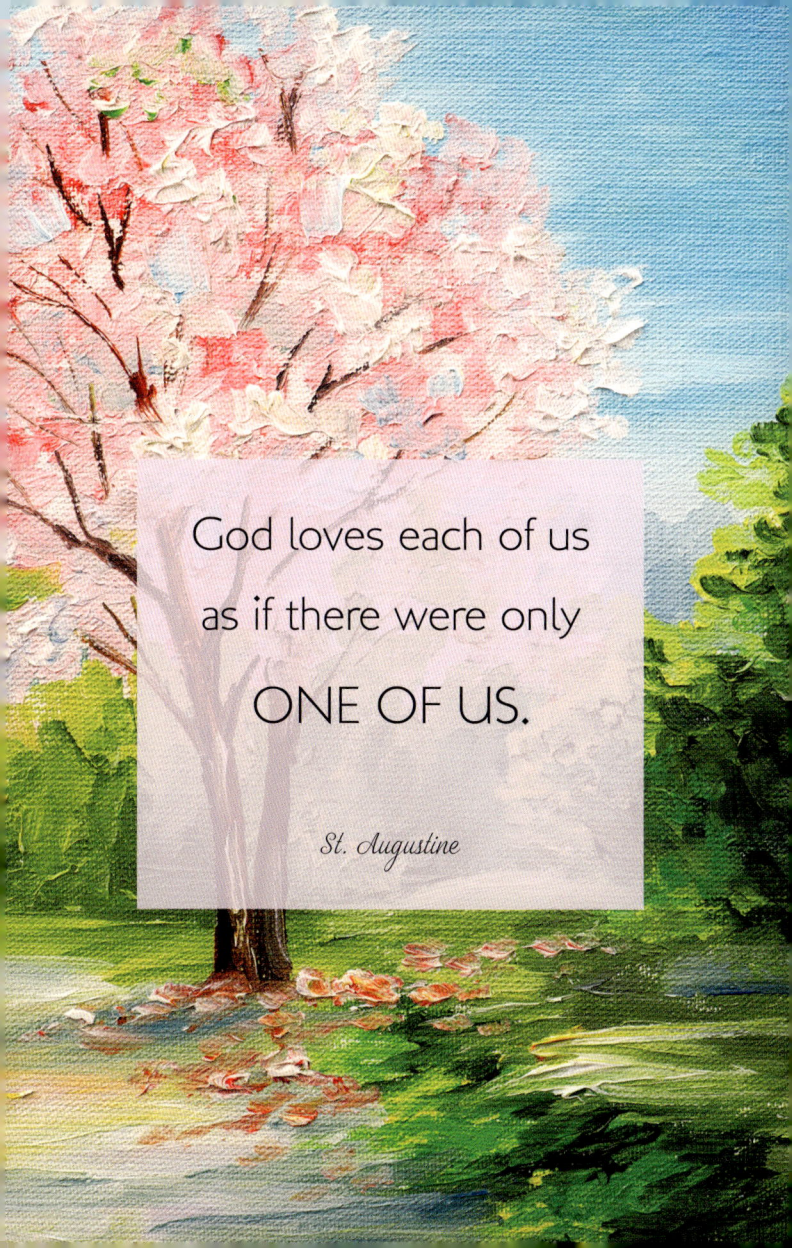

God loves each of us

as if there were only

ONE OF US.

St. Augustine

When I consider thy heavens,
the work of thy fingers,
the moon and the stars,
which thou hast ordained:

What is man,
that thou art mindful of him?
and the son of man,
that thou visitest him?

For thou hast made him
a little lower than the angels,
and hast crowned him
with glory and honour.

PSALM 8:3–5

We are not women of the world. We are women of God. And women of God will be among the greatest heroines of the 21st century. … We are unique because of our covenants, our spiritual privileges, and the responsibilities attached to both. We are endowed with power and gifted with the Holy Ghost. We have a living prophet to guide us, ordinances that bind us to the Lord and to each other, and the power of the priesthood in our midst. We understand where we stand in the great plan of happiness.

Sheri L. Dew

With the goodness of God

to desire our highest welfare,

the wisdom of God to plan it,

and the power of God to achieve it,

what do we lack?

Surely WE are the

MOST FAVORED

of all creatures.

Aiden Wilson Tozer

Unless the way we live draws us closer to our Heavenly Father and to our fellow men, there will be an enormous emptiness in our lives. God does notice us and watches over us, but it is usually through another person that He meets our needs. Therefore it is vital that we serve each other.

SPENCER W. KIMBALL

These things I have spoken
unto you, that in me
ye might have peace.
In the world ye shall
have tribulation:
but be of good cheer;
I have overcome the world.

John 16:32–33

He *values* us.

He *loves* us.

Each daughter of God

is *beloved* by Him

and He desires

to see us *all* succeed.

Neill F. Marriott

We must watch and pray, and look well to our walk and conversation, and live near to our God, that the love of this world may not choke the precious seed of truth, and feel ready, if necessary, to offer up all things, even life itself, for the Kingdom of Heaven's sake.

BRIGHAM YOUNG

Only fear the Lord, and serve him
in truth with all your heart:
for consider how great things
he hath done for you.

1 Samuel 12:24

*G*od's love melts everything else,
everything bad and everything mean
and everything despairing. Love conquers
everything, love conquers death,
but it must be God's love—a kind of love
that even loves its enemies: a love that
strides unperturbed like a warrior through
everything and can never be insulted or
hurt or despised, or thrown away,
and can never be repelled; a love that
strides through the world like a warrior
with the helmet of hope on its head.

Christoph Friedrich Blumhardt

But a faithful believer
will in all circumstances
meditate on the mercy
and fatherly goodness of God.

John Calvin

Once we surrender our mind
to God completely,
He will take care of us
in every way.

Sri Sathya Sai Baba

When we express thankfulness
to God and to his Son, Jesus Christ,
we base our faith and repentance
upon their forgiveness and their

goodness.

Robert D. Hales

Yea, I know that I am nothing;

as to my strength I am weak;

therefore I will not boast of myself,

but I will *boast of my God,*

for in his strength

I can do all things.

ALMA 26:11–12

We are children, perhaps, at the very moment when we know that it is as children that God loves us—not because we have deserved his love and not in spite of our undeserving; not because we try and not because we recognize the futility of our trying; but simply because he has chosen to love us. We are children because he is our father; and all of our efforts, fruitful and fruitless, to do good, to speak truth, to understand, are the efforts of children who, for all their precocity, are children still in that before we loved him, he loved us, as children, through Jesus Christ our Lord.

FREDERICK BUECHNER

As we step back and try to understand this love of God, we are astounded by its profound impact. At its center is the reality of a literal Father in Heaven whose love for His children knows no bounds. All truths, wisdom, power, goodness, and love He desires to share with His children, whom He created and sent to earth. He would have us reach up and know Him as a Father, as one who forgives, as a helper, as friend, as lawgiver—as one anxious to grant to every [person] the full opportunity of His love and potential and ultimately the blessing to one day become like Him. This love from Father in Heaven and its effects upon one of His children or the whole world is miraculous and contagious. He is constantly and everlastingly watching over us to lovingly and gently nudge us along.

James A. Paramore

We're all at different places on the path. But we can work together to help each other "press forward with a steadfastness in Christ, having a perfect brightness of hope, and a love of God and of all men" (2 Nephi 31:20).

Carole M. Stephens

If we will seek the grace of God,
He will come to our aid
and the aid of our loved ones
in times of need.
Let us obey the Lord
in all things and offer to Him
the ultimate sacrifice of
"a broken heart and a contrite
spirit" (3 Nephi 9:20).

Gene R. Cook

He that takes TRUTH
for his guide,
and DUTY for his end,
may safely trust
to GOD'S PROVIDENCE
to lead him aright.

BLAISE PASCAL

It makes the spirit soar to think
that the Creator of heaven and
earth could know us and love us
with a pure, eternal love.

JOSEPH B. WIRTHLIN

God waits for you to communicate
with Him. You have instant, direct
access to God. God loves mankind
so much, and in a very special sense
His children, that He has made
Himself available to you at all times.

WESLEY L. DUEWEL

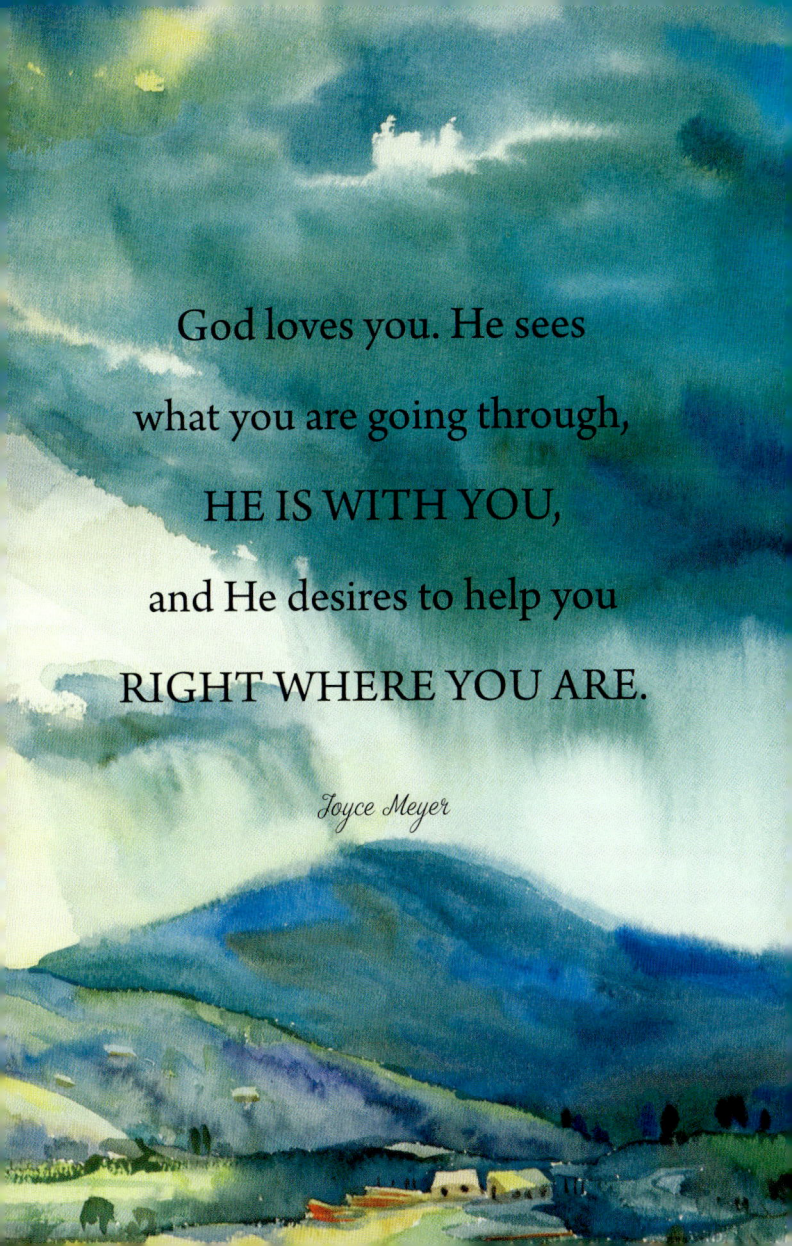

God loves you. He sees

what you are going through,

HE IS WITH YOU,

and He desires to help you

RIGHT WHERE YOU ARE.

Joyce Meyer

If the Lord be with us,

we have no cause of fear.

His eye is upon us,

His arm over us,

His ear open to our prayer—

His grace sufficient,

His promise unchangeable.

John Newton

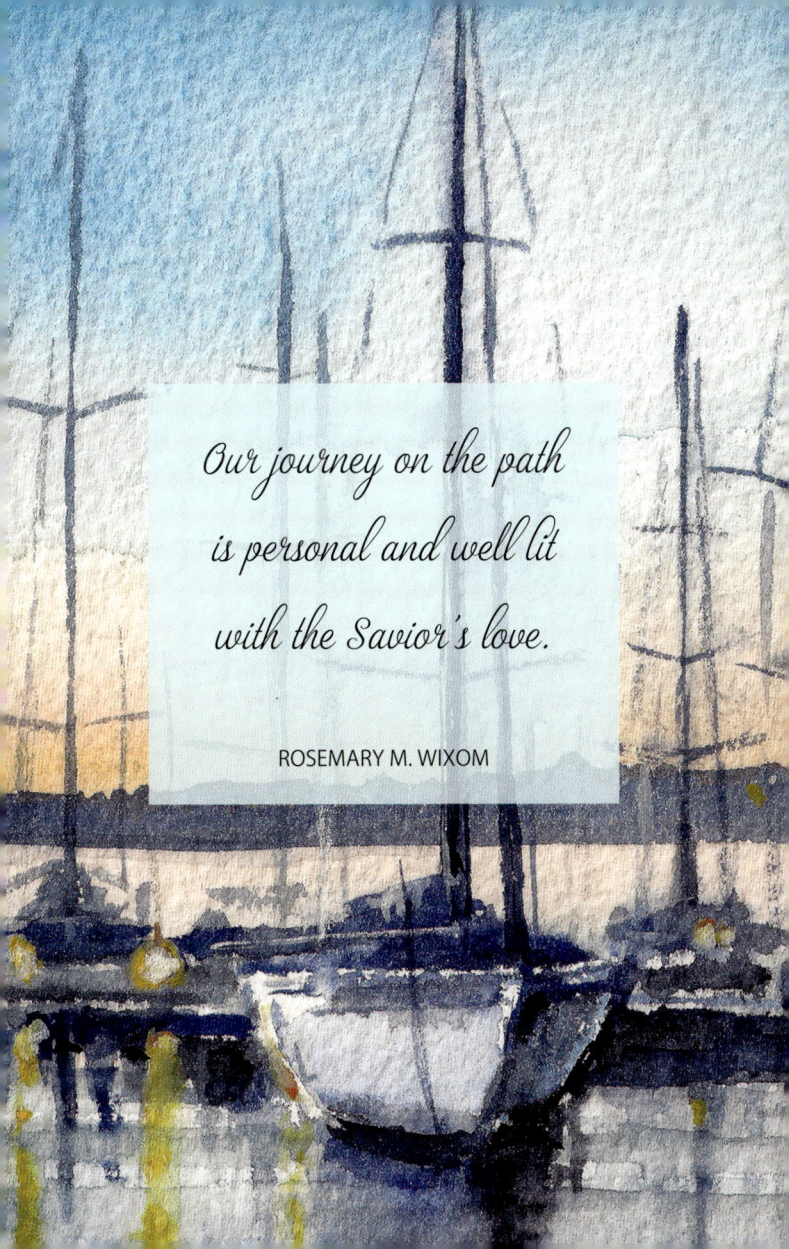

Our journey on the path
is personal and well lit
with the Savior's love.

ROSEMARY M. WIXOM

Happiness and comfort stream immediately from God himself, as light issues from the sun; and sometimes looks and darts itself into the meanest corners, while it forbears to visit the largest and the noblest rooms.

James H. Aughey

We sometimes, as women, have a tendency to be very critical of ourselves. During these times we need to seek the Spirit and ask, "Is this what the Lord wants me to think about myself, or is Satan trying to beat me down?" Remember the nature of our Heavenly Father, whose love is perfect and infinite. He wants to build us up, not tear us down.

Linda S. Reeves

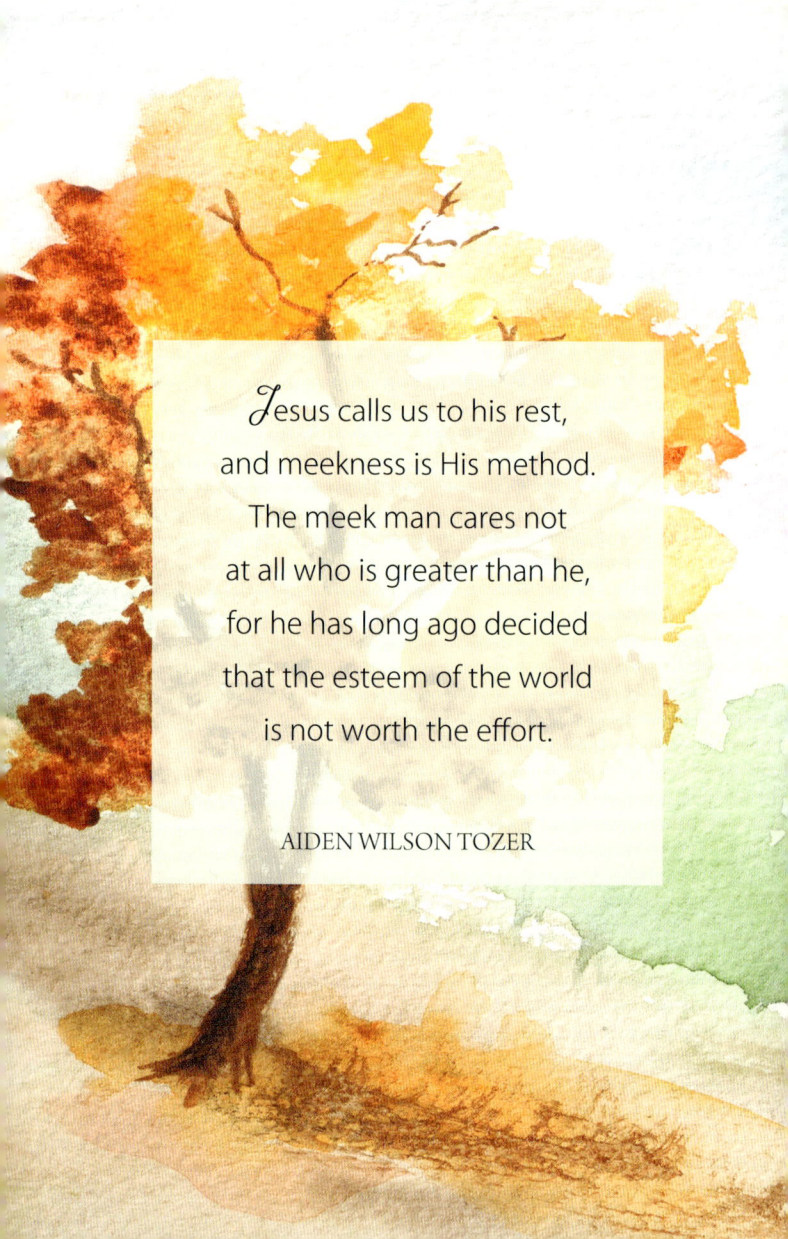

Jesus calls us to his rest,
and meekness is His method.
The meek man cares not
at all who is greater than he,
for he has long ago decided
that the esteem of the world
is not worth the effort.

AIDEN WILSON TOZER

In the many trials of life, when we feel abandoned and when sorrow, sin, disappointment, failure, and weakness make us less than we should ever be, there can come the healing salve of the unreserved love in the grace of God. It is a love that forgives and forgets, a love that lifts and blesses. It is a love that sustains a new beginning on a higher level and thereby continues "from grace to grace" (D&C 93:13).

JAMES E. FAUST

GOD KNOWS AND LOVES US ALL.
We are, every one of us, his daughters
and his sons, and whatever life's lessons
may have brought us, the promise is
still true: "If any of you lack wisdom, let
him ask of God, that giveth to all men
liberally, and upbraideth not; and it shall
be given him" (James 1:5).

Howard W. Hunter

O all ye that are *pure in heart*,

lift up your heads and receive

the pleasing word of God,

and *feast upon his love;*

for ye may, if your minds are firm,

forever.

JACOB 3:2

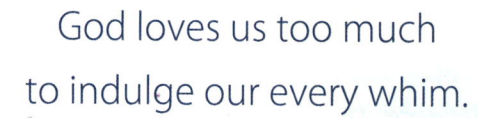

God loves us too much
to indulge our every whim.

MAX LUCADO

Men and women who are trying to make themselves happy in the possession of wealth or power will miss it, for nothing short of the Gospel of the Son of God can make the inhabitants of the earth happy, and prepare them to enjoy heaven here and hereafter.

Brigham Young

They may forget,

yet will I not forget thee.

Behold, I have

graven thee upon

the *palms of my hands.*

ISAIAH 49:15–16

I know that Jesus helps us
to be better women,
to be great women—
women who can
CHANGE THE WORLD.

M. Lucia Silva

He knows your sacrifices and
your sorrows. He hears your prayers.
His peace and rest will be yours as
you continue to wait upon Him in faith.

Robert D. Hales

Much of the major growth that is coming to the Church in the last days will come because many of the good women of the world (in whom there is often such an inner sense of spirituality) will be drawn to the Church in large numbers. This will happen to the degree that the women of the Church reflect righteousness and articulateness in their lives and to the degree that the women of the Church are seen as distinct and different—in happy ways—from the women of the world.

Spencer W. Kimball

SOURCES

Augustine, St. https://www.brainyquote.com/quotes/saint_augustine
    _105351.

Aughey, James H. https://www.christianquotes.info/top-quotes/18-
    amazing-quotes-about-gods-protection/.

Buechner, Frederick. *The Magnificent Defeat,* https://www.goodreads.
    com/quotes/tag/god-s-love?page=2.

Calvin, John. https://www.azquotes.com/quote/1102423.

Cook, Gene R. Quote on p. 16: "The Grace of the Lord," *New Era,* Dec. 1988
    (italics in original). Quote on p. 44: "Receiving Divine Assistance
    through the Grace of the Lord," Apr. 1993 General Conference.

Dew, Sheri L. "We Are Women of God," Oct. 1999 General Relief Society
    Meeting.

Duewel, Wesley L. https://www.christianquotes.info/top-quotes/17-
    amazing-quotes-about-gods-love/.

Faust, James E. "A Personal Relationship with the Savior," Oct. 1976
    General Conference.

Hales, Robert D. Quote on p. 39: "Gratitude for the Goodness of God,"
    Apr. 1992 General Conference. Quote on p. 59: "Waiting upon
    the Lord: Thy Will Be Done," Oct. 2011 General Conference.

Hunter, Howard W. "Blessed from on High," Oct. 1988 General Conference.

Jack, Elaine L. "Identity of a Young Woman," Oct. 1989 General Conference.

Julian of Norwich. https://www.azquotes.com/quote/510882.

Kimball, Spencer W. Quote on p. 31: "President Kimball Speaks Out on
    Service to Others," *New Era,* Mar. 1981. Quote on p. 60: "The Role
    of Righteous Women," 15 Sept. 1979, Women's Fireside at Salt Lake
    Tabernacle (address read by Camilla E. Kimball).

Kowalsaka, Mary Faustina. https://www.azquotes.com/quote/671366.

Lewis, C. S. https://quotefancy.com/quote/780169/C-S-Lewis.

Lucado, Max. Quote on page 13: *Grace for the Moment.* https://www.
    goodreads.com/quotes/465701. Quote on page 56: https://www.
    christianquotes.info/top-quotes/17-amazing-quotes-about-gods-love/.

Luther, Martin. https://www.azquotes.com/quote/963766.

Marriott, Neill F. "'Elect' Young Women Important to Work of Salvation,"
    Church News, 25 July 2013.

Meyer, Joyce. (https://joycemeyer.org/everydayanswers/ea-teachings/
    what-to-do-when-things-seem-hopeless).

Monson, Thomas S. "We Never Walk Alone," 28 Sept. 2013 General Relief
    Society Meeting.

Newton, John. https://www.christianquotes.info/top-quotes/18-amazing-
    quotes-about-gods-protection/.

Ogden, D. Kelly. *Where Jesus Walked: The Land and Culture of New Testament Times* (Salt Lake City: Deseret Book Co., 1991), 107.

Paramore, James A. "Love One Another," Apr. 1981 General Conference.

Pascal, Blaise. https://www.christianquotes.info/top-quotes/18-amazing-quotes-about-gods-protection/.

Reeves, Linda S. Quote on p. 24: "Claim the Blessing of Your Covenants," 28 Sept. 2013 General Relief Society Meeting. Quote on p. 51: Ibid.

Sai Baba, Sri Sathya. http://www.quotehd.com/quotes/sri-sathya-sai-baba-quote-once-we-surrender-our-mind-to-god-completely.

Scott, Richard G. "Trust in the Lord," Apr. 1989 General Conference.

Silva, M. Lucia. https://mybestlds.com/2015/02/24/12-great-quotes-from-young-women-leaders/.

Spurgeon, Charles Haddon. https://www.goodreads.com/quotes/1403154.

Stephens, Carole M. Quote on p. 14: "The Family Is of God," 28 Mar. 2015 General Women's Session. Quote on p. 43: "We Have Great Reason to Rejoice," 28 Sept. 2013 General Relief Society Meeting.

Tozer, Aiden Wilson. Quote on p. 2: https://www.azquotes.com/quote/943413. Quote on p. 30: https://www.azquotes.com/quote/573620. Quote on p. 52: https://www.goodreads.com/quotes/tag/christianity?page=3.

Warren, Rick. *The Purpose Driven Life: What on Earth Am I Here For?* (Grand Rapids, MI: Zondervan, 2002).

Wirthlin, Joseph B. "The Great Commandment," Oct. 2007 General Conference.

Wixom, Rosemary M. "Keeping Covenants Protects Us, Prepares Us, and Empowers Us," 29 Mar. 2014 General Women's Meeting.

Young, Brigham. Quote on p. 4: *Discourses of Brigham Young,* comp. John A. Widtsoe (Salt Lake City: Deseret Book Co., 1954), 305. Quote on p. 22: Ibid, 306. Quote on p. 34: Ibid, 314. Quote on p. 57: Ibid, 314.